TEEN WEALTH BLUEPRINT

The Ultimate Parent's Guide
to
Raising
Financially Smart and Independent Kids

Jennifer SJ

JSJ Group 7

ISBN-13: 9798300018832
ISBN-10: 1477123456

Cover design by: Art Painter
Library of Congress Control Number: 2018675309
Printed in the United States of America

CONTENTS

Teen Wealth Blueprint:
The Ultimate Parent's Guide
to
Raising
Financially Smart and Independent Kids

By:

Jennifer SJ

FOREWORD

We live in a time when young people have an unprecedented chance to shape their own futures and make meaningful contributions to the world long before they reach adulthood. But as parents, mentors, and guardians, we must provide them with the tools, guidance, and insights they need to maximize these opportunities.

In the years ahead, the financial landscape will continue to change, shaped by technology, innovation, and new working methods. Jobs and career paths that were once considered secure are being redefined, and new possibilities are opening in their place. Today's teens don't need to wait until they finish school to start gaining real-world experience; they can begin building skills, exploring business ideas, and even earning money through digital platforms, often with just a smartphone or laptop.

Teen Wealth is more than just a book about financial literacy. It's a resource to inspire teens and their parents to view money as a tool for freedom, responsibility, and creativity. This guide is filled with insights into budgeting, digital business ideas, and innovative saving strategies—all presented in a way that's accessible and engaging for teens. Each page encourages young readers to think critically about their relationship with money, understand its impact, and make decisions that align with their goals and values.

As a parent, you may be navigating these same financial principles yourself or revisiting them with fresh eyes alongside your teen. Wherever you are on your journey, remember that learning to build wealth, invest in oneself, and make responsible financial decisions is a skill that benefits every generation. In supporting our teens to become financially savvy, we're not only giving them a head start but equipping them with essential life skills.

Whether your teen is eager to dive into entrepreneurship, start freelancing, or wants to make better financial decisions, I hope this book becomes a valuable companion. Together, let's encourage them to embrace a future where they are financially independent and empowered to use their resources to create meaningful and fulfilling lives.

INTRODUCTION

In a rapidly changing world, one of the most important gifts we can give our teens is financial knowledge and independence. With the rise of the digital age, traditional career paths are evolving, and young people today have access to incredible opportunities that previous generations could only dream of. But for many teens, financial independence and smart money management remain intimidating—and understandably so. Between school, social lives, and planning for the future, navigating finances can feel overwhelming.

Teen Wealth empowers teens to explore the many pathways to financial independence, arming them with practical knowledge, skills, and strategies that go far beyond saving allowances or getting a part-time job. This guide is here to help parents and teens alike explore modern financial tools, learn the basics of budgeting, and uncover a world of digital business opportunities that teens can start right from their bedrooms. Whether freelance work, creating online content, or launching a small e-commerce business, today's teens have endless possibilities to earn, save, and grow their wealth.

This book isn't just about making money—it's about helping teens build a healthy relationship with money, instilling confidence, and preparing them for a future where financial literacy is essential. We'll cover how to think strategically about spending, saving, and investing alongside lessons on digital entrepreneurship, practical goal setting, and understanding the power of compounding growth.

With *Teen Wealth*, let's equip our teens to be financially aware, independent, and responsible. Together, we can help them build a foundation that will support them in making wise financial choices —today, tomorrow, and well into their adult lives.

CHAPTER 1: UNDERSTANDING FINANCIALLITERACY

The Importance of Financial Education

Financial education is a crucial component in teenagers' development, as it lays the foundation for their future financial decisions and overall economic well-being. Understanding money management principles empowers teens to make informed choices, avoid common pitfalls, and develop healthy financial habits. As they navigate through adolescence and adulthood, a solid grasp of economic concepts can significantly influence their ability to achieve personal and professional goals, fostering a sense of independence and responsibility.

Equipping teens with financial knowledge enables them to better understand the value of money and its role in their lives. This education encompasses various topics, including budgeting, saving, investing, and debt management. By learning these concepts early, teens can appreciate the importance of living within their means and the benefits of saving for future endeavors, such as higher education or entrepreneurial ventures. This foundation prepares them for financial stability and encourages them to think critically about their spending habits and economic decisions.

Moreover, financial literacy can inspire entrepreneurial aspirations among teenagers. As the world evolves, so do the opportunities available to young innovators and business-minded individuals. Understanding economic principles gives teens the confidence to explore entrepreneurship as a viable career path. They can learn to create budgets for business ideas, assess risks, and evaluate potential investment returns. This knowledge fosters creativity and innovation, as financially educated teens are more likely to pursue their passions and turn them into successful ventures.

In addition to personal benefits, financial education promotes a greater sense of community responsibility. Teens who understand financial concepts are likelier to engage in charitable giving, participate in community service, and advocate for financial literacy initiatives. As they become financially savvy, they can share their knowledge with peers and younger generations, fostering a culture of financial awareness and responsible money management within their communities. This ripple effect can contribute to a more financially literate society, benefiting everyone.

Finally, the importance of financial education cannot be overstated, especially in today's complex financial landscape. With the rise of digital currencies, online banking, and financial technology, the need for comprehensive financial education has never been more pressing. Parents play a vital role in this process by initiating conversations about money, encouraging open discussions about financial goals, and leading by example. By prioritizing financial education, parents can help their teens develop the skills and mindset necessary to navigate their financial futures confidently and successfully.

Key Concepts Every Teen Should Know

Understanding critical financial concepts is crucial for teenagers navigating the complexities of money management and entrepreneurship. One foundational concept is the difference between needs and wants. Teens should learn to identify essential expenses, such as food, clothing, and housing, versus non-essential items, like the latest gadgets or trendy clothing. By distinguishing between these two categories, teens can prioritize their spending and develop a more responsible approach to their finances, ultimately fostering a mindset that values long-term financial stability over short-term gratification.

Another essential concept is budgeting. Teens should be introduced to the basics of creating a budget, which involves tracking income, setting financial goals, and allocating funds for various expenses. Learning to budget empowers teens to take control of their finances and make informed decisions about managing their money. Parents can encourage their teens to practice budgeting by providing them with a monthly allowance or encouraging them to manage earnings from part-time jobs. This hands-on experience can lay the groundwork for healthy financial habits that will serve them well into adulthood.

Saving is another critical concept that every teen should grasp. Establishing a savings habit early on can significantly impact their financial future. Teens should be encouraged to set aside some of their income for emergencies, future purchases, or long-term goals like college or starting a business. Parents can help by introducing their teens to different savings accounts, such as high-yield or investment accounts. By understanding the value of saving and the benefits of compound interest, teens can be motivated to contribute to their savings consistently.

In addition to saving, understanding credit is essential for teens as they prepare to enter adulthood. Familiarizing them with how credit works, the importance of maintaining a good credit score, and the consequences of poor credit management can set them up for success. Parents can discuss credit cards, loans, and interest rates, emphasizing the importance of responsible borrowing. This knowledge will empower teens to make informed decisions about credit in their future financial dealings.

Finally, entrepreneurship is a vital concept that can inspire teens to take charge of their financial futures. Encouraging entrepreneurial thinking helps them to recognize opportunities, develop innovative solutions, and cultivate a strong work ethic. Parents can support their teens in exploring business ideas, participating in school clubs related to entrepreneurship, or even starting small ventures, such as lawn care or online shops. This hands-on experience teaches practical skills and instills confidence and a sense of responsibility, preparing them for the challenges and rewards of financial independence.

CHAPTER 2: SETTING FINANCIAL GOALS

Teaching Teens to Set SMART Goals

Teaching teens to set SMART goals is crucial in empowering them to take charge of their financial futures. The SMART framework stands for Specific, Measurable, Achievable, Relevant, and Time-bound. Each component is essential in helping teens articulate their aspirations clearly and effectively. By incorporating this methodology into their goal-setting practices, teens can gain clarity and motivation, making their ambitions more attainable and structured.

Specificity is the first element of SMART goals. When teens identify their goals, they should be encouraged to articulate them precisely. For instance, instead of saying, "I want to save money," a more specific goal would be, "I want to save $500 for a new laptop." This level of detail helps teens focus their efforts and resources on a defined target, eliminating ambiguity and enhancing their commitment to the goal.

Measurable goals allow teens to track their progress and celebrate milestones. By setting benchmarks, such as saving $100 monthly, teens can monitor their achievements and stay motivated. This measurable aspect also introduces them to accountability; checking their progress reinforces their responsibility towards their financial goals. Parents can assist by helping their teens create a chart or an app that tracks savings and expenditures, making the process interactive and engaging.

Achievable goals are about setting realistic expectations. While teens need to dream big, they should also consider whether their goals are attainable given their current circumstances. For example, if a teen wants to save for a car, they should realistically assess their income from part-time work and other sources. Parents can guide their teens in evaluating their capabilities and resources, ensuring that the goals are challenging yet reachable and fostering a sense of accomplishment as they progress.

The relevance of goals ensures that they align with a teen's values and long-term aspirations. Teens should be encouraged to reflect on why their goals matter to them personally. This connection enhances their motivation and reinforces the importance of prioritizing specific financial objectives over others. Finally, setting a time-bound element introduces urgency. Teens should aim to attach deadlines to their goals, such as saving the desired amount within six months. This structured timeline helps prevent procrastination and instills a sense of discipline in managing their financial habits, setting them on a path toward successful money management in the future.

Short-term vs. Long-term Goals

Short-term and long-term goals play a crucial role in the financial education of teens. Understanding the differences between these two goals can help young individuals develop a clear vision for their financial future. Short-term goals are typically defined as objectives that can be achieved within a year. They often include saving for a new phone, funding a weekend trip with friends, or purchasing a desired video game. These goals are usually specific and attainable, providing immediate gratification and a sense of accomplishment when completed.

On the other hand, long-term goals extend beyond one year and often require more significant planning and commitment. Long-term financial goals include saving for college, purchasing a car, or even starting a business. These goals involve more substantial money and can take several years to achieve. Setting long-term goals encourages teens to think about their future and instills the importance of saving and investing over time, which can lead to financial independence and stability.

Setting both short-term and long-term goals involves several steps. First, teens should identify their goals and establish a realistic timeline for each goal. Creating a budget can help determine how much money they need to save each month to reach their objectives. Parents can play a supportive role by helping their teens break down larger goals into smaller, manageable steps, making the journey less overwhelming and more structured.

Another important aspect of goal setting is the need for flexibility. Life circumstances can change, and financial priorities may shift. Both parents and teens need to review and adjust their goals as needed regularly. This adaptability will help teens learn to navigate unexpected challenges and maintain a positive outlook on their financial journey. Encouraging open discussions about financial goals fosters a supportive environment where teens can learn from their experiences and develop resilience.

Ultimately, balancing short-term and long-term goals is vital for financial success. Short-term goals provide immediate rewards and motivation, while long-term goals cultivate patience and strategic thinking. By understanding the significance of both goals, parents can better guide their teens in developing a solid financial foundation. This knowledge will not only empower young individuals to make informed decisions but also prepare them for a future where they can confidently achieve their aspirations and navigate the complexities of money management.

CHAPTER 3: BUDGETING BASICS

What is a Budget?

A budget is a financial plan that outlines expected income and expenses over a specific period, typically a month. It is a crucial tool for managing money effectively, allowing individuals to allocate resources toward necessary expenses, savings, and discretionary spending. Understanding the concept of a budget is essential for teens, as it lays the foundation for responsible financial habits that can last a lifetime. By learning to budget, teens can gain valuable skills to help them navigate their financial futures, especially as they earn their income through part-time jobs or entrepreneurial ventures.

Creating a budget involves several steps, starting with identifying all sources of income. This can include allowance, money earned from jobs, or income from a small business. Once income is established, the next step is to list all expected expenses. These expenses can be categorized into fixed costs, such as subscriptions or mandatory payments, and variable costs, such as entertainment or clothing. By clearly outlining income and expenses, teens can see where their money is going and make informed decisions about their spending habits.

One critical benefit of budgeting is that it encourages teens to prioritize their financial goals. Whether the goal is saving for a new gadget, funding a college education, or investing in a future business venture, a budget helps teens track their progress toward these objectives. By allocating a portion of their income to savings, teens learn the importance of delayed gratification and the value of setting aside money for future needs. This practice fosters a sense of responsibility and helps develop a mindset geared toward long-term financial success.

Moreover, budgeting can help teens develop essential skills such as discipline and self-control. By adhering to a budget, they learn to make choices about their spending, which can lead to a better understanding of the value of money. This experience is invaluable, especially in a consumer-driven society where instant gratification is often prioritized. Learning to say no to unnecessary expenses to achieve larger financial goals can empower teens and instill confidence in their decision-making abilities.

In conclusion, a budget is more than just a financial tool; it is a roadmap for achieving economic independence and success. For parents, teaching teens how to create and manage a budget can foster lifelong financial literacy and responsibility. By encouraging teens to engage in budgeting practices, parents can help them build a solid foundation for their financial future, equipping them with the skills needed to navigate the complexities of money management, entrepreneurship, and beyond.

Creating a Simple Budget

Creating a simple budget is an essential skill that empowers teens to control their finances. A budget is a roadmap that helps young individuals understand their income, expenses, and savings goals. The first step in creating a budget is to assess all sources of revenue. This may include allowances, part-time jobs, or entrepreneurial ventures for teens. By clearly identifying income, teens can grasp how much money they have available to manage.

Once income is established, the next step involves listing all expenses. This includes fixed costs, like subscriptions or transportation, and variable costs, like entertainment and dining out. Encouraging teens to track their spending for a month can provide valuable insights into their financial habits. This awareness allows for more informed decisions regarding where to cut back and how to allocate funds effectively.

After identifying income and expenses, parents can guide their teens in categorizing their spending. It's helpful to divide the costs into needs and wants. Needs are essential items like food, clothing, and school supplies, while wants include entertainment and luxury items. By distinguishing between these categories, teens can prioritize their spending and understand the importance of making choices that align with their financial goals.

Next, setting savings goals is crucial in the budgeting process. Parents should encourage their teens to allocate a portion of their income towards savings, whether for short-term goals like a new gadget or long-term aspirations such as college tuition. A good rule of thumb is 50/30/20: 50% for needs, 30% for wants, and 20% for savings. This framework can help teens develop a balanced approach to budgeting and instill the habit of saving early on.

Finally, regularly reviewing and adjusting the budget is vital for ongoing financial health. Encourage teens to revisit their budget monthly to reflect on their spending habits and make necessary adjustments. This practice helps them stay on track with their financial goals and teaches them the importance of adaptability in money management. By actively engaging in budgeting, teens can develop lifelong skills to serve them well in their entrepreneurial endeavors and personal financial journeys.

Tracking Spending

Tracking spending is a crucial skill for teens navigating their financial independence. By understanding where their money goes, they can make informed decisions and develop healthy financial habits that will benefit them throughout their lives. Encouraging teens to track their spending helps them gain insight into their financial priorities, identify unnecessary expenses, and create a budget that aligns with their goals. This practice not only fosters a sense of responsibility but also lays the groundwork for sound money management in the future.

One effective way for teens to track their spending is using a budgeting app or software designed for personal finance. Many of these tools come with user-friendly interfaces that simplify categorizing expenditures and monitoring spending habits. Parents can help their teens select an appropriate app, ensuring it meets their needs and offers features promoting engagement. Additionally, these tools often provide visual representations of spending trends, making it easier for teens to understand their financial behaviors at a glance.

Another method for tracking spending is through traditional pen-and-paper journaling. This approach can be especially beneficial for those who prefer a tactile experience or want to disconnect from screens. Teens can create a simple spending log, noting each purchase and its category, such as food, entertainment, or clothing. Regularly reviewing this log encourages reflection on spending choices and helps identify areas where they may want to cut back. This technique also reinforces the practice of mindfulness regarding financial decisions, teaching teens to think critically about their purchases.

Involving parents in the spending tracking process can enhance the learning experience for teens. Regular discussions about financial habits and goals can provide valuable insights and foster open communication about money management. Parents can share their experiences and lessons learned, creating a supportive environment where teens feel comfortable discussing their financial challenges. This collaborative approach strengthens the parent-teen relationship and ensures that teens have the knowledge and skills they need to succeed financially.

Ultimately, tracking spending is a foundational step toward financial literacy for teens. By instilling this practice early, parents can help their children develop essential money management skills that will serve them well into adulthood. As teens learn to monitor their expenses, they will be better prepared to set financial goals, save for future endeavors, and make informed decisions as they embark on their entrepreneurial journeys. Encouraging this habit will empower them to take control of their finances and build a solid foundation for their economic well-being.

CHAPTER 4: SAVING STRATEGIES

The Importance of Saving

Saving money is a fundamental skill that empowers teens to take control of their financial futures. In an era where consumerism is rampant and instant gratification is often prioritized, understanding the importance of saving can give young people a critical foundation for financial independence. By instilling the habit of saving early on, parents can help their teens learn to manage their resources effectively, set and achieve financial goals, and develop a sense of responsibility that will serve them throughout their lives.

One of the primary benefits of saving is that it cultivates a mindset of planning and foresight. Teens who save money learn to think critically about their expenses and prioritize their needs over wants. This ability to delay gratification is essential not only for personal finance but also for entrepreneurship. When young people save for future investments or business ideas, they understand the value of patience and strategic planning. This mindset can lead to better decision-making in their finances and potential business ventures.

Moreover, saving provides a safety net that can alleviate financial stress. Life is unpredictable, and savings allow teens to navigate unexpected expenses, such as car repairs or medical bills, without debt. When young people experience financial security, they are more likely to take calculated risks, such as starting a small business or pursuing further education. This sense of security fosters confidence and encourages them to explore opportunities they might otherwise shy away from due to financial anxiety.

In addition to immediate benefits, saving is also crucial for long-term wealth building. When teens learn to save regularly, they can take advantage of compound interest, which allows their money to grow over time. By understanding investing principles and the importance of starting early, parents can guide their teens toward making informed decisions about where to allocate their savings. This knowledge enhances their financial literacy and equips them with the tools necessary to build wealth and achieve financial independence in adulthood.

Finally, encouraging a culture of saving within the family can create a positive feedback loop. When parents model good saving habits and discuss money management, teens are likelier to adopt similar behaviors. Families can reinforce the value of teamwork and shared financial responsibility by setting savings goals together, such as a trip or a new gadget. This collaborative approach strengthens family bonds and empowers teens to become financially savvy adults who are well-equipped to manage their resources wisely.

Different Saving Methods

When it comes to saving money, teens have a variety of methods at their disposal, each offering unique advantages and drawbacks. One common approach is the traditional savings account, which allows teens to deposit their funds in a bank where they can earn interest over time. This method is particularly appealing due to its security and ease of access. Parents can assist their teens in opening these accounts, emphasizing the importance of regular deposits and monitoring their balances. Maintaining a savings account can instill a sense of responsibility as teens learn to manage their funds while watching their savings grow, albeit at a modest rate.

Another effective saving method is using a piggy bank or a personal savings jar. This approach is particularly beneficial for younger teens who may not yet have access to a bank account. By physically separating money into a designated container, teens can visualize their savings goals, whether for a new gadget, a special outing, or a more significant purchase. This hands-on method encourages the habit of saving small amounts consistently. Parents can enhance this experience by setting challenges or encouraging their teens to contribute a portion of any allowance or earnings to their savings jar.

For those looking to take a more entrepreneurial route, teens can benefit from creating a side hustle to boost their savings. This could involve offering services such as tutoring, lawn care, or even online freelancing. By earning their own money, teens not only have the opportunity to save but also develop essential skills such as budgeting and financial planning. Parents can support this initiative by helping their teens identify their strengths and interests, guiding them in marketing their services, and discussing how to allocate their earnings effectively.

Investing is another saving method that can be introduced to teens, albeit with careful consideration. While it may seem daunting, starting with small investments, such as stocks or mutual funds, can teach valuable lessons about the power of compound interest and the importance of long-term financial planning. Parents should explain the basics of investing, including the risks involved, and encourage their teens to research and select investments that align with their interests. This method builds wealth over time and fosters critical thinking and decision-making skills.

Finally, teens can explore digital savings tools and apps to simplify saving. Many financial institutions offer mobile banking options that allow users to set savings goals, track spending, and automate transfers to savings accounts. These digital tools can resonate well with tech-savvy teens, making saving more engaging and less tedious. Parents should encourage their teens to utilize these resources, discussing the importance of setting specific savings goals and regularly reviewing financial progress. By integrating technology into their saving habits, teens can develop a proactive approach to managing their finances that will serve them well into adulthood.

Setting Up a Savings Account

Setting up a savings account is a fundamental step in teaching teens about money management and fostering a habit of saving. Savings accounts help individuals save money while earning interest on their deposits. For parents, guiding teens through the process of opening a savings account provides an opportunity to instill valuable lessons about financial responsibility, budgeting, and planning for the future. This subchapter will outline the key considerations and steps in setting up a teen savings account.

The first step in setting up a savings account is to research different banking options available in your area. Parents should help their teens compare interest rates, fees, and features of various accounts. Many banks and credit unions offer special accounts tailored for young savers, often with lower costs and no minimum balance requirements. It is essential to consider whether the financial institution has online banking capabilities, mobile apps, and access to ATMs, as these features can enhance the banking experience for teens.

Once a suitable bank or credit union is identified, the next step is to gather the necessary documentation to open the account. Typically, the parent and the teen will need to provide identification, such as a driver's license or state ID for the parent and a school ID or Social Security number for the teen. Some banks may also require proof of address or a birth certificate. Parents should explain the importance of securing personal information and managing account credentials responsibly.

After the account is opened, discussing the importance of setting savings goals with your teen is crucial. Encouraging teens to identify specific savings objectives, such as purchasing a new smartphone, funding a school trip, or saving for college, will help them stay motivated. Parents can assist by creating a savings plan that outlines how much money needs to be saved each month to reach these goals. This practice teaches budgeting and reinforces the value of delayed gratification.

Finally, monitoring the savings account together can provide ongoing opportunities for financial education. Parents should encourage teens to check their account balances regularly, track their savings progress, and understand how interest accrues. Discussing the impact of spending habits on savings can help teens make informed decisions about their finances. By actively engaging in the savings process, parents can strengthen their teen's financial literacy and prepare them for a future of entrepreneurship and intelligent money management.

CHAPTER 5: INTRODUCTION TO INVESTING

What is Investing?

Investing is allocating resources, typically money, with the expectation of generating an income or profit. It involves purchasing assets such as stocks, bonds, real estate, or other financial instruments. The primary goal of investing is to build wealth over time, taking advantage of the potential for value growth. Understanding the basics of investing is crucial for teens as they begin to manage their finances and plan for their future. It is not solely about making money; it's also about making informed decisions that can lead to financial independence.

At its core, investing requires an understanding of risk and return. Investors must be aware that higher potential returns often come with higher risks. This means that while some investments might offer the possibility of substantial gains, they can also result in significant losses. Teaching teens about the risk-return relationship will help them make smarter investment choices. They should learn to analyze their risk tolerance, influenced by their financial goals, time horizon, and personal comfort with uncertainty.

One of the most common ways to invest is through the stock market. When individuals buy stocks, they purchase a share of ownership in a company. As the company grows and profits, the value of the shares can increase, allowing investors to sell them for a profit. Additionally, stocks can provide dividends and payments to shareholders from the company's earnings. Teens need to grasp how the stock market operates, as it is a significant part of the broader financial landscape and can be a powerful tool for building wealth over time.

Another critical aspect of investing is diversification. This strategy involves spreading investments across various assets to reduce risk. By not putting all their eggs in one basket, investors can protect themselves against the poor performance of a single investment. Teens should be encouraged to learn about different asset classes, such as stocks, bonds, mutual funds, and real estate, and consider how a diversified portfolio can help them achieve a balanced approach to investing.

Finally, the earlier one starts investing, the greater the potential for wealth accumulation due to the power of compound interest. This principle refers to earning interest on the initial principal and the accumulated interest from previous periods. For teens, investing early can lead to significant financial benefits in the long run. Parents can play a vital role by guiding their children in setting up investment accounts, understanding different investment vehicles, and encouraging habits that foster a long-term investment mindset. Through education and practical experience, teens can develop the skills to navigate investing confidently.

Types of Investments for Teens

When it comes to investing, teens have various options that can set them on a path to financial literacy and independence. One of the most accessible investments for young people is a savings account. Opening a high-yield savings account allows teens to earn interest on their deposits while learning the importance of saving. This foundational step teaches them how to manage their money and the benefits of accumulating wealth over time. Encouraging teens to deposit a portion of their allowance regularly or earnings helps instill a habit of saving that can last a lifetime.

Another popular investment choice for teenagers is stocks. With the advent of user-friendly trading platforms, investing in stocks has become more accessible than ever. Teens can begin by investing small amounts in fractional shares of companies they believe in or are familiar with, such as technology or consumer brands. This provides an educational experience about the stock market and encourages research and critical thinking. Parents can guide their teens in selecting stocks and understanding market trends, which can foster a sense of responsibility and ownership over their financial decisions.

Mutual and exchange-traded funds (ETFs) are suitable investment options for teens, offering a diversified approach that reduces risk. These funds pool money from multiple investors to buy a diverse range of stocks or bonds, making them an excellent way for young investors to gain exposure to various sectors of the economy. Investing in mutual funds or ETFs allows teens to learn about diversification and the importance of not putting all their eggs in one basket. Parents can help teens explore funds that align with their interests and financial goals, promoting informed decision-making.

Real estate can be another exciting avenue for teenage investors, primarily through Real Estate Investment Trusts (REITs). REITs allow individuals to invest in real estate without the need to manage properties directly. This type of investment can appeal to teens interested in the housing market while providing a practical introduction to passive income. Learning about how real estate appreciation works and the impact of market trends can inspire teens to think about long-term investments and financial strategies.

Lastly, investing in their entrepreneurial ventures can be one of the most empowering investment forms for teens. Starting a small business or side hustle allows young people to apply their knowledge and creativity in a practical setting. This type of investment has the potential for financial return, enriches their life experiences, and builds essential skills such as budgeting, marketing, and customer service. Parents can support this endeavor by encouraging their teens to develop business plans and offering guidance on managing their finances, thus fostering a mindset geared towards entrepreneurship and financial success.

Risk vs. Reward

Risk vs. Reward is a fundamental concept in finance and entrepreneurship, especially relevant for teens who are beginning to navigate their financial futures. Understanding this balance is crucial for making informed investment decisions, business ventures, and personal finance. The essence of risk versus reward is that higher potential returns often come with more significant risks. Recognizing this relationship can lead to more strategic and thoughtful choices for young individuals eager to start their entrepreneurial journeys or manage their money effectively.

When discussing risk, defining what it means in a financial context is essential. Risk refers to the possibility of losing some or all of an investment. For teens, this could manifest in various ways, such as investing in stocks, starting a small business, or even spending money on a new gadget that may or may not yield satisfaction. Understanding the nature of these risks is the first step toward making prudent decisions.

Encouraging teens to evaluate potential pitfalls and prepare for possible setbacks can build resilience and a realistic approach to entrepreneurship.

Conversely, the reward is the potential gain from taking on risk. This could be financial profits from a business venture, increased knowledge from a failed experiment, or personal growth from overcoming challenges. Parents can support their teens in recognizing that while the prospect of failure can be daunting, the lessons learned from such experiences are invaluable. By fostering an environment where calculated risks are encouraged, parents can help their children develop a mindset that views setbacks as growth opportunities rather than definitive endpoints.

One practical way to illustrate the risk versus reward dynamic is through real-life examples. Parents might share stories of successful entrepreneurs who took significant risks that eventually paid off, such as starting a business with little initial capital or investing in a volatile market. Conversely, discussing instances where risks did not result in success can be equally beneficial, emphasizing the importance of learning and adapting. These narratives can provide a balanced perspective and help teens understand that every successful entrepreneur has faced obstacles and made mistakes.

Teaching teens about risk versus reward instills a sense of responsibility and strategic thinking in their financial decisions. Parents should encourage open discussions about economic choices, helping their children to weigh potential risks against expected rewards. This prepares them for future financial endeavors and cultivates a mindset that values informed decision-making. By equipping teens with the tools to assess risks and rewards, parents can empower them to become financially savvy individuals capable of navigating the complexities of the entrepreneurial landscape.

CHAPTER 6: ENTREPRENEURSHIP 101

What is Entrepreneurship?

Entrepreneurship refers to starting and operating a business to make a profit. It encompasses a range of activities, including identifying a market need, developing a product or service to meet that need, and taking on the risks associated with running a business. Entrepreneurship is not limited to starting new companies; it can also involve innovating within existing organizations or finding new ways to deliver value. Understanding the fundamentals of entrepreneurship can empower teens to think creatively about their skills and interests while fostering a sense of responsibility and independence.

At its core, entrepreneurship is driven by the desire to solve problems and create value. Young entrepreneurs often identify gaps in the market or inefficiencies in existing services and seek to address them. This problem-solving mindset is essential for success in the business world and is a skill that can be developed over time. Parents can encourage teens to explore their passions and think critically about how they might turn those interests into viable business opportunities. This exploration can lead to a greater understanding of market dynamics and the importance of customer feedback in refining ideas.

Financial literacy is a crucial component of entrepreneurship. Understanding basic economic concepts such as budgeting, pricing, and cash flow management is vital for anyone starting a business. Teens should learn to calculate costs, set prices, and track their income and expenses. This knowledge not only aids in running a successful business but also instills good money management habits that will benefit them in personal finance. Parents can support their teens in this learning process by discussing financial topics openly and providing resources that enhance their understanding of money.

Moreover, entrepreneurship fosters essential life skills that extend beyond the business realm. Skills such as communication, teamwork, and adaptability are cultivated by starting and managing a business. Teens learn how to negotiate, market their ideas, and interact with customers, which can enhance their confidence and social skills. These experiences prepare them for future endeavors, whether in the workplace or in their personal lives. Parents can help by encouraging their teens to take on leadership roles in group projects or community activities, allowing them to practice these skills in real-world settings.

Finally, the landscape of entrepreneurship is continually evolving, particularly with advancements in technology and shifts in consumer behavior. Today, young entrepreneurs have unprecedented access to resources and platforms that can help them launch their ventures. The rise of social media, e-commerce, and digital marketing has democratized starting a business, making it more accessible than ever for teens. Parents should encourage their children to embrace these tools while emphasizing the importance of ethical business practices and social responsibility. By nurturing an entrepreneurial spirit, parents can equip their teens with the skills and mindset needed to thrive in an ever-changing economic landscape.

Identifying Opportunities

Identifying opportunities is crucial for parents and teens in cultivating financial literacy and entrepreneurial spirit. The first step in this process is encouraging teens to observe their surroundings and identify problems that need solutions. Teach them to look for gaps in the market or inefficiencies in everyday life. This could be anything from lacking healthy snack options at school to needing a tutoring service in a specific subject. By recognizing these challenges, teens can begin brainstorming potential business ideas that address these needs, laying the groundwork for future entrepreneurial endeavors.

Once teens have identified potential problems, parents can assist them in conducting market research. This involves gathering information about the target audience, existing competitors, and market trends. Encourage your teen to create surveys or conduct interviews to gather insights from peers and community members. This research validates their ideas and helps them understand the importance of knowing their audience. By engaging in this process, teens learn to assess the viability of their concepts and develop a more informed approach to entrepreneurship.

In addition to traditional market research, parents can introduce their teens to online resources that provide valuable insights into emerging trends and opportunities. Websites, social media platforms, and industry reports can offer inspiration and highlight areas ripe for innovation. Encourage teens to follow entrepreneurs and thought leaders in fields of interest, as this exposure can spark new ideas and motivate them to think creatively about potential business ventures. Understanding the digital landscape allows them to identify opportunities that align with their passions and strengths.

Networking is another critical component in identifying opportunities. Parents should encourage their teens to seek local business events, workshops, and entrepreneurial meetups. These gatherings provide valuable knowledge and allow teens to connect with like-minded individuals and seasoned entrepreneurs. Building a network can lead to mentorship opportunities, partnerships, and potential customers. By actively engaging in their communities, teens can broaden their horizons and discover opportunities that might not be apparent in their immediate environment.

Finally, cultivating a mindset that embraces failure as a learning opportunity is essential for identifying and seizing opportunities. Encourage your teen to take calculated risks and view setbacks as valuable lessons rather than discouragements. This resilience will empower them to continue exploring new ideas and avenues, even when faced with challenges. By fostering an environment where experimentation is celebrated, parents can help teens develop the confidence and adaptability needed to navigate the ever-changing landscape of entrepreneurship and money management.

Developing a Business Idea

Developing a business idea is a crucial first step in the entrepreneurial journey. For teens, this process can be both exciting and challenging. Understanding that a viable business idea often stems from personal interests, skills, and community needs is essential. Encouraging teens to explore their passions can help spark innovative ideas. Parents can support this exploration by engaging their teens in conversations about what they enjoy doing, what problems they see around them, and how they might provide solutions.

Research plays a vital role in refining a business idea. Teens should be encouraged to conduct market research to identify potential customers and competitors. This involves gathering information about existing products or services, understanding consumer preferences, and evaluating pricing strategies. Parents can assist by guiding their teens to various resources such as online surveys, social media platforms, and local community feedback. This research will not only validate the business idea but also instill a sense of confidence in their entrepreneurial aspirations.

Once a promising idea is identified, developing a business plan is next. A business plan outlines its mission, vision, objectives, and strategies for achieving them. Parents should emphasize the importance of setting realistic goals and milestones. This plan should also include a budget highlighting potential costs and revenue streams. By involving teens in this planning process, parents can teach them valuable lessons in financial management and strategic thinking, which are essential for future success.

Prototyping and testing the business idea are crucial next steps. This phase allows teens to create a minimum viable product or service and gather feedback from potential customers. Parents can encourage teens to seek peers, family, and mentors constructive criticism. This feedback loop helps improve the product and fosters resilience as teens learn to adapt and pivot based on real-world input. Parents need to remind their teens that failure is often part of the entrepreneurial process and can lead to better outcomes in the long run.

Finally, launching the business is an exciting culmination of the idea development process. Parents can assist by helping their teens create a marketing strategy to promote their business. This could involve leveraging social media, designing flyers, or organizing local events. Teens must understand the importance of building a brand and connecting with their audience. By guiding their teens through each step of this journey, parents can help cultivate a spirit of entrepreneurship that empowers their children and equips them with essential life skills in money management and business acumen.

Here are some ideas on digital business opportunities teens can start:

1. **Social Media Management**: Social media-savvy teens can start a business managing social media accounts for local businesses, influencers, or even family friends. They can help design posts, create content calendars, and engage with followers, developing valuable marketing skills.

2. **Content Creation and Blogging**: Starting a blog, YouTube channel, or podcast allows teens to share their passions, whether gaming, fashion, or science, while building a following. As they gain traction, they can monetize through sponsorships, affiliate marketing, and ads.

3. **Freelance Design and Video Editing**: Teens with a knack for design can offer services on platforms like Fiverr or Upwork. Designing logos and graphics or editing videos for other content creators can be a great entry point into freelance work.

4. **Digital Tutoring and Course Creation**: With many people learning online, teens can offer tutoring in subjects they excel at, like math or languages, or create digital courses and guides. These can be sold through websites like Teachable or Gumroad.

5. **Print-on-Demand Products**: Teens can design items like t-shirts, mugs, or phone cases and sell them through print-on-demand platforms like Redbubble, TeeSpring,

or Etsy. This is a low-cost way to explore e-commerce and entrepreneurship with minimal inventory risk.

6. **Affiliate Marketing**: Teens with a good online following or a blog can earn by promoting products they believe in, using affiliate links from companies like Amazon Associates or niche brands. They earn commissions when followers make purchases through their links.

7. **App or Game Development**: For teens interested in coding, creating a simple app or game can be a great project that may also generate revenue. They can start with small, creative projects, using platforms like the App Store or Google Play to publish and promote them.

8. **Online Reselling**: Teens can purchase discounted products, such as vintage clothing or collector items, and resell them on platforms like eBay, Depop, or Poshmark. This is a hands-on way for them to learn about marketing, pricing, and customer service.

CHAPTER 7: BUILDING A BUSINESS PLAN

Critical Components of a Business Plan

A business plan is an essential document that outlines the roadmap for a new venture, serving as both a guide for the entrepreneur and a tool for securing funding. For teens interested in entrepreneurship, understanding the key components of a business plan can provide a strong foundation for their future endeavors. A well-structured business plan helps clarify business ideas and ensures that young entrepreneurs think critically about their goals and strategies.

The executive summary is the first component of a business plan and serves as an overview of the entire document. It should briefly describe the business concept, the target market, and the unique value proposition. This is an opportunity for teens to articulate their vision clearly and compellingly. An engaging executive summary can capture the interest of potential investors or mentors and set the tone for the rest of the plan, making it a crucial element to get right.

Next, the market analysis provides insights into the industry landscape and target market. This section should include market trends, customer demographics, and the competitive environment. Teens should research their chosen industry, identifying potential customers and competitors. Understanding these factors enables young entrepreneurs to position their businesses effectively, allowing them to tailor their products or services to meet specific customer needs and preferences.

The marketing and sales strategy outlines how the business will attract and retain customers. This component should detail the marketing channels, promotional tactics, and sales processes the teen entrepreneur intends to use. Young business owners must think creatively about their marketing strategies, leveraging social media and digital platforms that resonate with their peers. A strong marketing plan can enhance visibility and drive sales, which are critical for business success.

Finally, the financial projections section is vital for demonstrating the business idea's viability. This includes projected income statements, cash flow statements, and balance sheets for the first few years of operation. Understanding basic financial concepts is crucial for teens, as it helps them anticipate expenses, revenue, and profitability. By preparing realistic financial projections, young entrepreneurs can assess their business's potential and communicate its financial health to potential investors or stakeholders.

Financial Projections

Financial projections are essential for anyone looking to navigate the world of entrepreneurship and money management, especially for teens who are just beginning to understand how to manage their finances effectively. Creating financial projections involves estimating future income, expenses, and overall financial health over a specific period. For teens, this practice not only helps set realistic financial goals but also teaches valuable budgeting and financial planning skills. Parents can play a crucial role in guiding their teens through this process, ensuring they grasp the importance of forecasting their financial future.

To begin with, teens should learn how to create a simple income statement. This statement outlines expected revenues from various sources, such as part-time jobs, allowances, or earnings from entrepreneurial ventures. Teens can set achievable financial goals by estimating how much money they can realistically earn. Parents can encourage teens to record their income sources and amounts over a few months to gain insights into their earning potential. This initial step lays the groundwork for more detailed financial projections and fosters a sense of accountability in managing their income.

Next, teens must understand their expenses. Teaching them to categorize expenses into fixed and variable costs helps them see where their money goes. Fixed costs include regular payments like subscriptions or memberships, while variable costs may include discretionary spending on entertainment, clothes, or hobbies. By tracking these expenses, teens can identify areas where they might cut back, thus maximizing their savings. Parents can assist by providing tools such as budgeting apps or spreadsheets that help their teens visualize their spending patterns, promoting healthier financial habits.

Once income and expenses are outlined, the next step is to project future financial scenarios. This involves potential raises, increased allowance, or additional revenue from new ventures. It also requires predicting future expenses, including anticipated costs for school, extracurricular activities, or personal projects. Encouraging teens to create best-case, worst-case, and most likely scenarios can enhance their critical thinking and decision-making skills. This exercise teaches them to prepare for uncertainties and understand the importance of flexibility in financial planning.

Lastly, regularly reviewing and adjusting financial projections is vital for ongoing financial literacy. As circumstances change—whether through new job opportunities, unexpected expenses, or shifts in personal interests—teens should learn to adapt their projections accordingly. This process can be a family activity, where parents and teens come together to review financial goals and make necessary adjustments. By fostering open discussions about money management and financial planning, parents can empower their teens to take charge of their financial futures, equipping them with the tools they need for lifelong financial success.

Marketing Strategies

In today's competitive landscape, marketing strategies play a crucial role in the success of any entrepreneurial venture, especially for teens looking to establish their businesses. Understanding marketing fundamentals can empower parents and teens to navigate the complexities of reaching potential customers effectively. Marketing is about identifying and satisfying customer needs while building a brand that resonates with the target audience. Parents can facilitate discussions about the importance of market research, helping teens learn how to gather insights about their target demographic, including preferences, behaviors, and current trends. This foundational knowledge can set the stage for informed decision-making throughout the business journey.

One effective marketing strategy for teens is leveraging social media platforms. With their familiarity and comfort in using these platforms, teens can create engaging content that showcases their products or services. Parents should encourage teens to develop a content calendar and explore various formats, such as videos, stories, and posts highlighting unique selling points. By understanding the nuances of each platform, including Instagram, TikTok, and Facebook, teens can tailor their marketing efforts to reach their audience effectively. Additionally, parents can assist in setting guidelines for responsible social media use, ensuring that teens maintain a professional online presence while still being authentic.

Another powerful marketing strategy is to harness the power of word-of-mouth marketing. Encouraging teens to engage with their peers and build a community around their business can lead to organic growth. Parents can help by guiding their teens on creating referral programs, offering incentives for customer recommendations, or even hosting small local events. This approach not only fosters a sense of belonging but also builds trust within the community. By understanding the impact of personal recommendations, teens can appreciate the value of relationships and networking in growing their businesses.

Email marketing is another strategy that can be particularly effective for teens. Although it may seem less appealing to younger audiences, a well-executed email campaign can yield significant results. Parents should guide their teens in building an email list of interested customers and crafting compelling messages that provide value. This could include exclusive offers, updates on new products, or informative content that aligns with the interests of their audience. Teaching teens how to analyze open rates and engagement metrics can help them refine their approach and understand the importance of continuous improvement in their marketing efforts.

Finally, collaborating with other young entrepreneurs can amplify marketing efforts. Parents can encourage teens to seek partnerships with peers with complementary products or services. Joint promotions, social media takeovers, or co-hosted events can broaden their reach and introduce their brands to new audiences. By working together, teens can learn valuable lessons about collaboration, resource sharing, and the benefits of mutual support in entrepreneurship. This strategy enhances their marketing capabilities and cultivates a spirit of teamwork and innovation as they navigate their entrepreneurial journeys.

CHAPTER 8: EARNING MONEY AS A TEEN

Part-time Jobs and Side Hustles

Part-time jobs and side hustles offer valuable opportunities for teens to earn money while gaining essential skills and experience. Many young people seek ways to contribute financially to their families or save for personal goals. Part-time positions, whether in retail, food service, or tutoring, provide an income and a taste of responsibility and independence. These jobs help teens understand the importance of time management, customer service, and teamwork, all of which are vital skills in the workplace.

In addition to traditional part-time jobs, side hustles have become increasingly popular among teens. With the rise of technology and the internet, young people can explore various avenues to generate income beyond conventional employment. Options like freelancing, selling handmade crafts online, or offering services like pet sitting or lawn care allow teens to tap into their interests and talents. These entrepreneurial experiences can be enriching, fostering creativity and encouraging teens to think critically about how they can turn their passions into profit.

Parents are crucial in guiding their teens through finding and managing part-time jobs or side hustles. Open discussions about financial goals, work-life balance, and the importance of work ethics can help teens make informed decisions about their employment choices. It is equally important to encourage them to set realistic expectations regarding their work hours and responsibilities. This guidance helps teens navigate their jobs and instills a sense of accountability and maturity to serve them well in their future endeavors.

When teens engage in part-time work or side hustles, they also learn the importance of budgeting and saving. Earning their own money gives them a firsthand understanding of financial concepts such as income, expenses, and savings goals. Parents can assist by helping their teens create a budget based on their earnings and teaching them how to allocate funds for necessities, savings, and discretionary spending. This practical experience lays the foundation for sound money management habits that will benefit them in adulthood.

Finally, the experiences gained from part-time jobs and side hustles can significantly impact a teen's future career. Young people who explore various roles and industries often discover their interests and strengths, which can guide their educational and professional choices. Furthermore, the skills acquired through these experiences—such as communication, problem-solving, and resilience—are invaluable assets in any career. Parents can help their teens build a strong foundation for financial independence and career success by supporting their teens in pursuing these opportunities.

Freelancing and Gig Economy

Freelancing and the gig economy have emerged as significant opportunities for teens seeking financial independence and developing essential skills. Unlike traditional jobs, freelancing allows individuals to offer their services on a project basis, enabling them to work on tasks that align with their interests and strengths. The gig economy encompasses various short-term jobs, often facilitated through online platforms, which can be a great entry point for teens to earn money while balancing their academic responsibilities. This dynamic work environment encourages creativity, adaptability, and self-discipline, providing invaluable experiences that can shape their future career paths.

Understanding the freelancing landscape is crucial for parents to guide their teens in this endeavor. Many platforms cater specifically to young freelancers, allowing them to showcase their graphic design, writing, programming, and digital marketing skills. Encouraging teens to explore these opportunities can help them identify their passions and develop a portfolio demonstrating their capabilities. Parents should also emphasize the importance of professionalism and communication when working with clients, as these soft skills can significantly impact a teen's success in the gig economy.

Time management is another critical aspect of freelancing that teens must learn to navigate. Balancing schoolwork, extracurricular activities, and freelance projects can be challenging, but developing practical time management skills will serve them well throughout their lives. Parents can support their teens by helping them create schedules that allocate time for each commitment while ensuring they set realistic deadlines for their freelance projects. This practice not only cultivates responsibility but also instills a strong work ethic essential in any career.

Financial literacy is vital for teens venturing into freelancing. Independent workers must manage their earnings, track expenses, and understand essential tax obligations. Parents should take the opportunity to educate their teens about budgeting and saving and the importance of maintaining accurate income records. Setting up a separate bank account for freelance earnings can also help teens learn about money management and prepare for potential future investments or expenses related to their work.

Ultimately, the gig economy offers a unique platform for teens to explore their entrepreneurial spirit. By engaging in freelance work, they can learn valuable lessons about resilience, problem-solving, and self-promotion. Parents play a pivotal role in this journey by providing guidance, resources, and encouragement. As teens navigate the world of freelancing, they not only build their financial skills but also gain confidence and independence that will benefit them in their future endeavors.

Here are some popular platforms where teens can start freelancing, with specific examples based on the type of work they're interested in:

1. Fiverr

- **Best for Beginners and those looking to offer services such as** graphic design, video editing, writing, voiceovers, and virtual assistance.
- **How it Works**: Freelancers create "gigs" (service listings) with set prices, allowing clients to browse and hire them directly. Teens can start with more straightforward tasks and gradually increase their prices as they gain experience.

2. Upwork

- **Best For** Various services, including writing, web development, social media management, and virtual assistance.
- **How it Works**: Freelancers create a profile and submit proposals for projects posted by clients. To build a portfolio, teens can search for short-term jobs or ongoing work opportunities.

3. Freelancer.com

- **Best for Teens looking for flexible work in design, writing, data entry, and marketing fields**.

- **How it Works**: Similar to Upwork, teens can submit project bids. There are also contests where they can submit entries for things like logo design and earn money if their entry is selected.

4. Behance (by Adobe)

- **Best For** Portfolio building, particularly for graphic design, photography, and illustration.
- **How it Works**: Teens can create a portfolio to showcase their work and connect with clients who browse profiles looking for creative talent. Behance can be a valuable platform for attracting clients and getting noticed by creative professionals.

5. 99designs

- **Best For**: Graphic designers interested in logo, website, or branding design.
- **How it Works**: Designers can enter contests to showcase their skills or get hired directly for projects. This site is a good option for teens skilled in graphic design who want to gain experience through project-based work.

6. PeoplePerHour

- **Best For** Teens offers writing, design, marketing, and software development services.
- **How it Works**: Freelancers create "Hourlies" (hourly job listings) or submit proposals to clients who post job listings. It's beginner-friendly and offers a variety of projects across skill levels.

7. Voices.com

- **Best For** Teens interested in voiceover work.
- **How it Works**: Freelancers can create a profile and audition for voiceover jobs in areas like audiobooks, video games, or commercials. This platform requires some investment in audio quality, but it's a great place to break into voiceover work.

8. Tutor.com or Chegg Tutors

- **Best For** Academic tutoring in subjects like math, science, or English.
- **How it Works**: Teens can sign up as tutors if they meet the age requirements (some sites require tutors to be 18+ or have specific qualifications). These platforms connect tutors with students who need help.

9. Etsy (for Print-on-Demand and Digital Products)

- **Best For** Selling handmade, print-on-demand, or digital products (like templates, digital art, or printable planners).
- **How it Works**: Teens can set up a shop to sell custom-designed items or digital downloads. This is ideal for those who want to create products and potentially automate their earnings.

10. Rev

- **Best For** Transcription, captioning, and subtitling jobs.
- **How it Works**: Freelancers are paid per audio minute transcribed. Rev is open to beginners and offers training, making it a good starting point for teens with strong typing skills.

11. ACX (Audiobook Creation Exchange)

- **Best For** Audiobook narration for teens with a clear voice.
- **How it Works**: Freelancers audition for audiobook narration roles for self-published authors. Payment is typically per project, or a royalty share, and it's a popular choice for aspiring voiceover artists.

12. LinkedIn

- **Best For**: Building a professional network for a variety of skills.
- **How it Works**: Teens can create profiles, connect with professionals, showcase their skills, and apply for freelance jobs. It's a more professional space to promote services and find freelance work directly from businesses.

13. Social Media Platforms (Instagram, Facebook, TikTok)

- **Best For** Freelancers looking to promote services directly, such as graphic design, social media management, or photography.
- **How it Works**: Teens can create business profiles showcasing their work and reach potential clients by posting examples, client testimonials, and interactive stories or reels.

These platforms offer a range of opportunities for teens to get started with freelancing, build a portfolio, and gain valuable work experience.

Entrepreneurship and Starting a Business

Entrepreneurship is a powerful avenue for teens to explore their interests while developing essential life skills. Starting a business allows young people to express their creativity and teaches them valuable lessons about responsibility, financial management, and problem-solving. Parents can play a crucial role in guiding their teens through this journey, helping them understand the foundational principles of entrepreneurship and its impact on their future.

When considering entrepreneurship, teens should begin by identifying their passions and interests. This self-reflection helps them recognize what they enjoy doing and where they can add value in the marketplace. A business idea could stem from a hobby, a skill, or a gap in the market they have observed. Encouraging teens to brainstorm and research potential business concepts fosters creativity and innovation, laying the groundwork for a successful venture.

Once a business idea has been established, the next step involves creating a solid business plan. This document is a roadmap outlining the business's goals, target audience, marketing strategies, and financial projections. Parents can assist their teens in developing this plan by discussing the importance of setting realistic objectives and understanding the competition. A well-thought-out business plan guides the entrepreneur and helps secure funding if needed.

Financial literacy is a vital component of entrepreneurship. Teens must learn how to budget, manage expenses, and keep track of profits and losses. Parents can teach their children basic accounting principles and the importance of maintaining accurate financial records. Understanding cash flow and how to reinvest profits into the business will empower teens to make informed decisions that can lead to sustainable growth.

Finally, resilience is critical in the entrepreneurial journey. Teen entrepreneurs will undoubtedly face challenges and setbacks and must learn how to adapt and persevere. Parents can encourage a growth mindset, emphasizing that failures are opportunities for learning and growth. By fostering an environment where teens feel supported and motivated, parents can help instill the confidence needed to navigate the ups and downs of running a business, ultimately preparing them for future success in their financial endeavors.

CHAPTER 9: UNDERSTANDING CREDIT

What is Credit?

Credit is a financial concept that refers to the ability to borrow money or access goods and services with the understanding that payment will be made in the future. It is a crucial part of the financial system and plays a significant role in individuals' finances. Understanding credit is essential for parents and teens, as it impacts significant life decisions such as buying a car, applying for student loans, or renting an apartment. Credit allows individuals to make purchases when they don't have the total amount of cash available upfront, promoting financial flexibility while requiring responsibility in repayment.

Credit operates on the principle of trust. Lenders provide funds based on the belief that the borrower will repay the borrowed amount and any agreed-upon interest. This trust is established through a credit score, a numerical representation of a person's creditworthiness. Credit scores are calculated based on various factors, including payment history, the amount of debt owed, length of credit history, new credit inquiries, and types of credit used. A higher credit score indicates a lower risk to lenders, making it easier to secure loans and obtain favorable interest rates.

Understanding credit is particularly important for teens as they approach adulthood. Many young people establish their credit history by opening a bank account, getting a credit card, or taking out a student loan. These early financial decisions can significantly influence their credit scores later.

Parents can help guide their teens through this process by discussing the implications of each choice and encouraging responsible financial habits, such as making timely payments and keeping debt levels manageable.

Building credit is a gradual process that requires patience and discipline. Teens should be educated on how to monitor their credit reports, which can be obtained for free annually from the major credit bureaus. By reviewing their reports, they can identify any inaccuracies or fraudulent activities that could negatively impact their credit score. Furthermore, parents should emphasize the importance of using credit wisely, such as only borrowing what can be repaid and avoiding impulse purchases that may lead to financial strain.

In conclusion, every teen should understand credit is an essential part of financial literacy. It affects their future economic opportunities and stability. Parents play a critical role in helping their children navigate the world of credit, equipping them with the knowledge and skills to make informed decisions. By fostering discussions about credit, teaching responsible borrowing practices, and encouraging regular monitoring of credit scores, parents can empower their teens to build a solid financial foundation for their future.

The Importance of a Good Credit Score

A good credit score is an essential aspect of financial health that can significantly impact a teenager's future. As parents, understanding the importance of credit scores and conveying this knowledge to your teens can set the foundation for their financial independence. A credit score is a numerical representation of a person's creditworthiness derived from their credit history, which includes payment history, amounts owed, length of credit history, new credit, and types of credit used. For teens, establishing a positive credit history early can lead to better financial opportunities in adulthood.

One of the primary advantages of a good credit score is access to favorable loan terms. When teens transition into adulthood and seek to finance their education, purchase a car, or buy a home, lenders will evaluate their credit scores to assess the risk of lending to them. A higher credit score often translates into lower interest rates, which can save thousands of dollars over the life of a loan. By instilling a good understanding of credit management in teens, parents can help them secure better financial products that align with their entrepreneurial aspirations.

Additionally, a solid credit score can enhance job prospects. Many employers conduct background checks that include credit reports, especially for positions that involve financial responsibilities. A favorable credit history can reflect personal responsibility and reliability, which employers value. Teaching teens how to maintain good credit practices, such as paying bills on time and managing debt, can improve their credit scores and chances of securing desirable job opportunities in the future.

Moreover, a good credit score provides a safety net in emergencies. Unexpected expenses, such as medical bills or car repairs, can arise anytime. With a strong credit score, teens can access credit cards or loans more efficiently, enabling them to handle these situations without falling into financial distress. This ability to manage unforeseen circumstances fosters a sense of security and confidence in their financial decision-making.

Finally, understanding credit scores cultivates a sense of financial responsibility among teens. As they learn about the implications of credit usage, they become more aware of their spending habits and the importance of saving. Encouraging teens to check their credit scores regularly, understand the factors that influence them, and develop healthy financial habits will empower them to take control of their financial future. By prioritizing credit education, parents play a crucial role in equipping their children with the skills necessary to navigate the complexities of the financial world.

How to Build Credit as a Teen

Building credit as a teen is a crucial step toward financial independence and responsibility. Understanding the basics of credit can empower young individuals to make informed decisions that will benefit them in the long run. Parents play an essential role in guiding their teens through this process, offering early support and education about the importance of establishing a good credit history. Teens who grasp these concepts can navigate their financial futures with confidence.

One of the first steps in building credit is obtaining a secured credit card. This card type requires a cash deposit as collateral, which serves as the credit limit. For example, if a teen deposits $300, they can spend up to that amount. This method allows them to use credit in a controlled manner while minimizing the risk of going into debt. Parents need to help their teens research different secured card options, paying close attention to fees and terms to ensure they select a card that aligns with their financial goals.

Another effective way for teens to build credit is by becoming authorized users on their parents' credit cards. This arrangement allows them to purchase using the card while benefiting from the primary cardholder's established credit history. Parents should ensure they manage their credit responsibly, as any late payments or high balances can negatively affect their credit score and their teen. This strategy provides a practical learning experience for teens about managing credit and the importance of on-time payments.

Establishing a budget is also an essential aspect of building credit. Teens should learn to track spending and understand the importance of living within their means. Parents can assist by encouraging their teens to create a simple budget that accounts for income from part-time jobs, allowances, and any gifts. Teaching teens about budgeting fosters responsible financial habits and helps them prepare for the financial responsibilities of credit use, such as paying off balances in full each month.

Finally, teens must monitor their credit reports regularly. Many credit reporting agencies offer free reports that can be accessed once a year. Parents should encourage teens to review these reports for accuracy and understand the factors influencing their credit scores. By instilling the habit of monitoring credit at a young age, parents can help their teens develop a proactive approach to managing their financial health, setting the stage for a strong credit profile as they move into adulthood.

CHAPTER 10: RESPONSIBLE SPENDING

Needs vs. Wants

Understanding the difference between needs and wants is fundamental for financial literacy, especially for teens beginning to manage their money. Needs are essential items necessary for survival and day-to-day functioning. These include food, shelter, clothing, and healthcare. On the other hand, wants are non-essential items that enhance quality of life but are not crucial for survival. Examples of wants include designer clothes, the latest smartphone, or frequent dining out. Teaching teens to distinguish between these two categories is critical in developing sound money management skills.

Teens can make more informed financial decisions when they understand needs versus wants. This distinction helps them prioritize their spending and allocate their resources effectively. For instance, if a teen has a limited budget, understanding that they need to buy groceries over a new video game can help them avoid impulsive purchases that could lead to financial strain. Encouraging teens to create budgets that categorize their spending can further reinforce this understanding. It empowers them to allocate their money towards fulfilling their essential needs while managing their wants responsibly.

Another critical aspect of needs versus wants is the influence of marketing and peer pressure. Teens are often bombarded with advertisements promoting the latest trends and products, creating a blurred line between what they need and want. Parents can play a crucial role in guiding their teens through these influences by discussing marketing strategies and helping them critically assess the necessity of certain purchases. This dialogue not only aids in discerning needs from wants but also cultivates critical thinking skills essential for entrepreneurship and financial success.

Moreover, understanding the distinction between needs and wants can foster a sense of gratitude and appreciation among teens. When they learn to recognize and prioritize their essential needs, they may better appreciate what they have. This mindset can lead to more thoughtful spending habits and an inclination to save for meaningful goals rather than immediate gratification. Parents can encourage this by involving teens in discussions about family finances and the value of saving for future needs, such as education or starting a business.

In conclusion, teaching teens the difference between needs and wants is a vital lesson in financial literacy that contributes to their overall development as financially savvy individuals. Parents can help their teens build a solid foundation for making wise financial choices by equipping them with the knowledge and skills to manage their finances effectively. This understanding will aid them in personal finance and prepare them for entrepreneurial endeavors, where discerning between essential investments and unnecessary expenditures is crucial for success.

Impulse Buying and How to Avoid It

Impulse buying is common among teens, who may be more susceptible to marketing tactics and peer influence. This phenomenon occurs when individuals make unplanned purchases driven by emotions rather than necessity. For teens, the allure of social media advertisements, in-store displays, and peer pressure can lead to impulsive decisions that detract from their long-term financial goals. Understanding impulse buying triggers is crucial for parents and teens to cultivate a healthier relationship with money.

One of the main factors contributing to impulse buying is the emotional response associated with shopping. Teens often experience a range of emotions, from excitement to boredom, which can prompt them to seek immediate gratification through purchases. Recognizing these emotional triggers is essential for developing strategies to curb impulsive behavior. Parents can help their teens identify situations where they feel compelled to buy, encouraging reflective practices that allow them to pause and evaluate their desires before purchasing.

Another significant aspect of impulse buying is the influence of marketing tactics. Advertisers are skilled at creating a sense of urgency and exclusivity, mainly through social media platforms that resonate with younger audiences. Parents should educate their teens about these marketing strategies, emphasizing the importance of critical thinking when faced with enticing offers. Discussions about the difference between wants and needs can empower teens to make informed decisions, ultimately reducing the likelihood of impulse purchases.

Creating a budget is a practical way to manage spending and prevent impulse buying. Parents can work with their teens to establish a monthly allowance or savings plan that allocates funds for discretionary spending. By setting clear financial boundaries, teens can learn to prioritize spending and make conscious choices about where their money goes. Encouraging teens to track their expenses can also provide valuable insights into their spending habits, helping them recognize patterns that lead to impulsive purchases.

Lastly, fostering a culture of saving rather than spending can significantly impact a teen's financial behavior. Parents can encourage teens to set savings goals for items they want rather than succumbing to immediate desires. This practice promotes patience and teaches the value of delayed gratification. By instilling these principles, parents can help their teens develop a strong foundation in money management, reducing the likelihood of impulse buying and guiding them toward more responsible financial decision-making.

Making Informed Purchases

Making informed purchases is a crucial skill that can significantly impact a teen's financial future. Understanding the value of money and the importance of making thoughtful buying decisions lays the foundation for responsible spending habits. As parents, guiding teens through this process can help them develop critical thinking skills regarding their finances. By instilling the principles of informed purchasing, parents can encourage their children to become savvy consumers who prioritize value over impulse.

The first step in making informed purchases is researching products and services before committing to any expenditure. Encourage teens to compare different brands, prices, and features. This can involve reading product reviews, seeking peer opinions, and utilizing online comparison tools. By engaging in this research, teens learn to evaluate their options critically and avoid falling for marketing gimmicks that may lead to regretful purchases. Teaching them to look for credible sources of information will empower them to make choices based on facts rather than emotions.

Budgeting plays a pivotal role in informed purchasing decisions. Parents can guide their teens in creating a personal budget that accounts for their income, savings goals, and necessary expenses. This practice helps teens understand how to allocate their funds wisely and highlights the importance of saving for larger purchases. When teens operate within a budget, they become more conscientious about their spending habits and are less likely to make impulsive decisions that can derail their financial goals.

Another essential aspect of making informed purchases is understanding value versus cost. Parents should teach their teens to assess whether a product justifies its price based on its quality, longevity, and utility. For instance, investing in a higher-quality item that lasts longer may be more economical in the long run than buying cheaper items that require frequent replacement. This understanding fosters a mindset where teens prioritize long-term satisfaction over short-term gratification, encouraging them to be more discerning consumers.

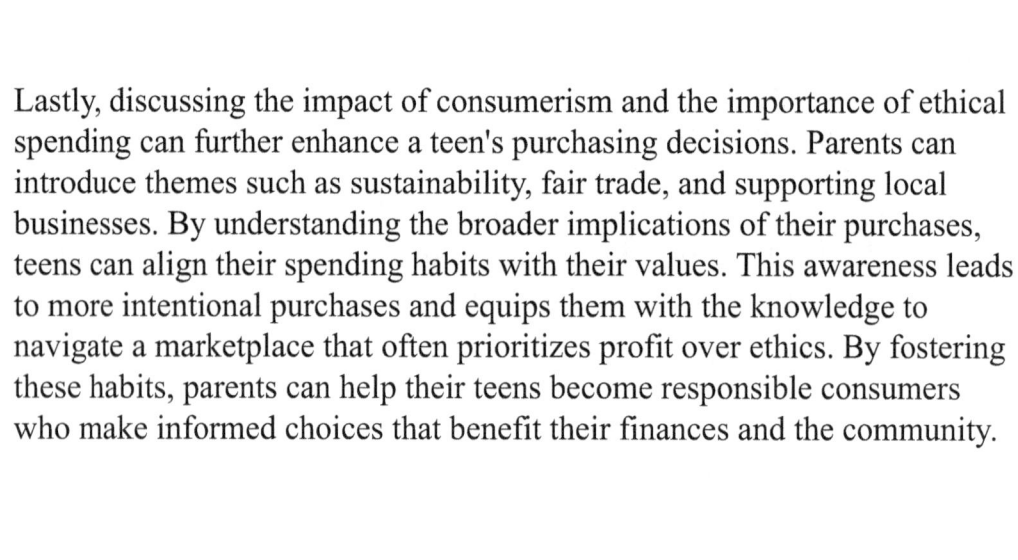

Lastly, discussing the impact of consumerism and the importance of ethical spending can further enhance a teen's purchasing decisions. Parents can introduce themes such as sustainability, fair trade, and supporting local businesses. By understanding the broader implications of their purchases, teens can align their spending habits with their values. This awareness leads to more intentional purchases and equips them with the knowledge to navigate a marketplace that often prioritizes profit over ethics. By fostering these habits, parents can help their teens become responsible consumers who make informed choices that benefit their finances and the community.

CHAPTER 11: TEACHING TEENS ABOUT TAXES

Understanding Taxes

Understanding taxes is a crucial aspect of financial literacy that teenagers should learn about, especially as they begin earning their own money. Taxes are a percentage of income that individuals must pay to the government to fund public services and infrastructure for teens starting to earn through part-time jobs, internships, or entrepreneurial ventures; understanding how taxes work can help them make informed financial decisions and avoid surprises when tax season arrives.

The first step in understanding taxes is recognizing the different types of taxes that may apply. Income tax is most commonly levied on earnings from work or business activities. Depending on where you live, there may also be state or local taxes that apply. There are other taxes, such as sales tax, property tax, and capital gains tax, which may be relevant for teens engaging in activities like selling products online or investing in stocks. Understanding these categories can help teens develop a broader view of their financial responsibilities.

Filing taxes can seem daunting, but it is an essential skill for financial independence. Teens should learn about filing taxes, including the importance of keeping accurate records of their income and expenses throughout the year. Parents can guide their teens by showing them how to organize receipts, pay stubs, and bank statements. This organization will simplify the filing process and ensure they can claim any deductions or credits they may be eligible for, ultimately reducing their tax liability.

Another critical aspect of taxes is understanding tax brackets and how they impact take-home pay. The tax system is progressive, meaning that different portions of income are taxed at different rates. This structure can affect how much money a teen will take home after taxes are deducted from their paycheck. By educating teens on how tax brackets work, parents can help them make better decisions about their earnings, such as whether to take on extra gigs or how to budget effectively for their expenses.

Finally, parents should encourage their teens to view taxes not just as a burden but as a civic responsibility. Taxes contribute to essential services like education, healthcare, and infrastructure that benefit everyone in the community. By fostering a positive attitude toward taxes, parents can help their teens appreciate their societal role and understand the importance of being responsible citizens. This mindset will prepare them for their financial futures and instill values that prioritize community and social responsibility.

How Taxes Affect Income

Understanding how taxes affect income is crucial for parents and teens, especially in entrepreneurship and money management. Taxes are a mandatory contribution to government revenue, levied on personal income, corporate profits, sales, and other financial transactions. For young entrepreneurs, recognizing the implications of taxes on their earnings can help them make informed decisions about their business ventures and personal finances. This knowledge equips teens to understand that the money they earn is not entirely theirs to keep and encourages responsible financial planning.

When teens start earning money through a part-time job, freelance work, or a small business, they must grasp the concept of taxable income. Taxable income is the portion of income that is subject to taxation after deductions and exemptions. Young entrepreneurs need to keep accurate records of their earnings and expenses. This practice not only helps in understanding their actual income but also assists in calculating their tax obligations. Teens should be aware that different sources of income may be taxed differently, and keeping detailed records will ease the process when tax season arrives.

Another crucial aspect is the various types of taxes that may apply to their earnings. Income tax is the most commonly thought of, but there are also self-employment taxes, sales taxes, and sometimes even local taxes to consider. For instance, if a teen operates a small business selling handmade crafts, they may need to collect sales tax from customers and remit it to the government. Understanding these tax responsibilities is essential, as failing to comply can result in penalties that could impact their budding business and overall financial health.

Moreover, the impact of taxes on income can significantly influence how much money teens have available for savings and reinvestment in their ventures. By understanding tax brackets and how income is taxed at different levels, teens can strategize their earnings to maximize their take-home pay. This could involve deciding how much to work, whether to reinvest in their business or how to save for future goals. Teaching teens about tax strategies, such as contributing to retirement accounts or other tax-advantaged savings options, can lead to healthier financial habits in the long run.

Lastly, fostering a positive attitude towards taxes can help teens view this aspect of money management as a civic duty rather than a burden. Parents can encourage discussions about how taxes contribute to community services, infrastructure, and public goods that benefit everyone. By framing taxes in this light, teens can develop a sense of responsibility and appreciation for their role in society. This perspective helps them manage their finances effectively and prepares them for a future where they can contribute positively to their communities.

Filing Taxes for the First Time

Filing taxes for the first time can be a daunting experience for teens and their parents. Understanding the basics of the tax system is crucial for young individuals, especially those who are beginning to earn money through part-time jobs, freelance work, or entrepreneurial ventures. Parents play a vital role in guiding their teens through this process, ensuring they grasp the importance of meeting tax obligations and the potential benefits of filing. Familiarizing teens with fundamental concepts, such as income, deductions, and credits, can empower them to approach tax season confidently.

The first step in filing taxes is determining whether your teen needs to file a return. Generally, if a teenager earns above a certain income threshold from wages or self-employment, they must file a tax return. For the tax year 2023, that threshold typically hovers around $13,850 for earned income. Different thresholds apply if your teen has unearned income, such as interest or dividends. Parents should encourage their teens to keep track of all earnings throughout the year to ensure accurate reporting when tax season arrives.

Once it's established that your teen needs to file, the next step is to gather the necessary documentation. This includes W-2 forms from employers, 1099 forms for freelance work, and any other relevant financial documents. Parents can assist by demonstrating how to organize and store these documents throughout the year. Teaching teens to maintain accurate records simplifies the tax filing process and instills good financial habits that will serve them well in the future.

Choosing the proper method for filing taxes is another critical consideration. Teens can opt for various options, including filing manually using paper forms or utilizing online tax software. Many tax preparation services offer free filing for those with simple returns, which can be beneficial for first-time filers. Parents should discuss the pros and cons of each method with their teens, highlighting the importance of accuracy and the potential for e-filing to expedite refunds. This is also an excellent opportunity to teach them the importance of reviewing their returns for errors before submission.

Finally, once the taxes are filed, it is essential to discuss the outcome, whether it results in a refund or a tax bill. If your teen receives a refund, it can be a valuable lesson in budgeting and saving for future expenses, such as college or a personal project. Conversely, if they owe taxes, this is an opportunity to discuss financial planning and the importance of setting aside money for tax obligations in the future. By guiding teens through the entire tax process, parents can help them develop a solid understanding of their financial responsibilities and set the stage for a financially literate adulthood.

CHAPTER 12: THE ROLE OF TECHNOLOGY IN MONEY MANAGEMENT

Financial Apps for Teens

In today's digital age, financial literacy is more important than ever, especially for teens beginning to navigate their financial responsibilities. Financial apps designed specifically for young people can serve as essential tools in teaching money management skills. These applications not only help teens learn about budgeting, saving, and investing, but they also provide practical experiences that can foster a sense of financial independence. Parents should explore these options with their teens to ensure they understand how to use them effectively.

One popular category of financial apps for teens is budgeting applications. These apps allow users to track their spending, categorize expenses, and set savings goals. By engaging with a budgeting app, teens can gain insights into their spending habits and learn the importance of living within their means. Some apps even include features that enable users to set alerts for overspending or to monitor their progress toward financial goals. This hands-on approach helps instill essential budgeting skills that will benefit them throughout their lives.

Savings apps are another crucial resource for teens. Many of these applications encourage users to save by offering incentives, such as rounding up purchases to the nearest dollar and depositing the difference into a savings account. This "save as you spend" model can make saving less daunting and more achievable for young users. By incorporating gamification elements, such as rewards for reaching savings milestones, these apps can motivate teens to prioritize saving and develop a habit that will serve them well into adulthood.

Investing in apps tailored for young people also transforms how teens approach their finances. These platforms often feature user-friendly interfaces and educational content that explain the basics of investing, including stocks, bonds, and ETFs. Some apps even allow users to start investing with small amounts of money, making it accessible for teens who may not have significant savings. By learning about investing early, teens can cultivate a growth mindset regarding their money and understand the power of compound interest over time.

Finally, many financial apps for teens include educational resources to enhance their understanding of personal finance. These resources may include articles, videos, quizzes, or interactive modules covering credit, debt, and financial planning. By utilizing these educational features, parents can guide their teens in developing a well-rounded understanding of economic concepts. This knowledge prepares them for future financial decisions and empowers them to become confident and informed adults who can navigate the complexities of their financial lives.

Online Banking and Security

Online banking has become integral to managing finances for teens and their parents. With the rise of digital platforms, young people have unprecedented access to their accounts, enabling them to monitor their spending, track savings, and even invest. However, this convenience also highlights the importance of understanding the security measures necessary to protect sensitive financial information. Parents play a crucial role in educating their teens about the potential risks and how to navigate them safely.

One of the primary concerns in online banking is the threat of cybercrime, which can manifest in various forms, such as phishing scams, identity theft, and account hacking. Teens, often more accustomed to digital interactions, may underestimate the need for caution. Parents must discuss these risks openly, emphasizing recognizing suspicious emails, messages, or links. Encouraging teens to verify sources and think critically about the information they encounter online can significantly reduce their vulnerability to these threats.

Another critical aspect of online banking security is solid passwords and authentication methods. Teens should be taught to create complex passwords that are difficult to guess and to avoid using the same password across multiple accounts. Additionally, parents can introduce their teens to the concept of two-factor authentication, which adds an extra layer of security by requiring a second form of verification before accessing accounts. These practices can empower teens to take control of their financial security and understand the importance of safeguarding their personal information.

Parents should also encourage their teens to monitor their banking activity regularly. Young individuals can quickly identify unauthorized charges or discrepancies by reviewing their account statements and transaction histories. This practice enhances their awareness of their financial situation and instills a sense of responsibility and vigilance. Parents can guide their teens on how to report suspicious activities to their bank and the importance of acting swiftly to mitigate potential damages.

Lastly, fostering open communication about online banking and security can strengthen trust between parents and teens. Parents should feel comfortable discussing their experiences with online banking, including any challenges they faced and how they overcame them. Sharing stories of success and caution can serve as valuable lessons for teens. By creating an environment where questions and discussions about money management are encouraged, parents can equip their teens with the knowledge and skills necessary to navigate the digital financial landscape confidently and securely.

Using Technology to Create Budgets

Creating a budget is a fundamental skill for financial management. In today's digital age, technology offers a variety of tools to make this process easier and more effective for teens. Parents can play a crucial role in guiding their children through budgeting by introducing them to various technological resources that can simplify financial planning. These tools help teens understand the importance of budgeting and empower them to take control of their finances early on.

One of the most accessible tools for budgeting is budgeting apps, designed to help users track their income, expenses, and savings goals. Popular applications like Mint, YNAB (You Need a Budget), and Pocket Guard allow teens to input their financial information and categorize their spending. These apps often provide visual representations of spending habits, which can help teens identify areas where they can cut back. By engaging with these tools, teens learn to monitor their finances in real time, fostering a sense of responsibility and accountability.

In addition to budgeting apps, many banks offer online banking tools to aid the budgeting process. These platforms typically include features such as spending analysis, alerts for low balances, and goal-setting options. Parents can encourage teens to set up bank accounts and utilize these features to develop a deeper understanding of money management. This practical experience helps teens become comfortable with financial terminology and instills confidence in their ability to manage money independently.

Another valuable resource is online courses and tutorials focused on financial literacy. Many organizations and educational platforms provide free or low-cost resources that teach budgeting, saving, and investing. Parents can explore these options with their teens to supplement their learning. These courses can spark meaningful discussions about financial goals and priorities and make informed financial decisions. This collaborative approach can enhance the learning experience and strengthen the parent-child relationship.

Parents can encourage their teens to create digital spreadsheets or use financial software like Microsoft Excel or Google Sheets for more personalized budget tracking. By designing their budget templates, teens can tailor their economic plans to suit their needs and preferences. This hands-on experience reinforces their learning and allows them to experiment with different budgeting methods. As they navigate the world of technology and finance, teens will develop essential skills that will serve them well into adulthood, setting a solid foundation for their financial futures.

CHAPTER 13:
DISCUSSING MONEY AS
A FAMILY

Creating a Family Financial Plan

Creating a family financial plan is essential in teaching teens about responsible money management and entrepreneurship. A well-structured financial plan serves as a roadmap for the family's financial future, helping to align goals, track expenses, and allocate resources efficiently. Involving teens in this process empowers them with knowledge and fosters a sense of responsibility and ownership over their financial decisions. This subchapter will explore the critical components of developing a family financial plan and how parents can engage their children.

The first step in creating a family financial plan is establishing clear financial goals. These goals vary widely, from saving for a family vacation to funding education or even starting a business. Parents should involve their teens in discussions about these goals, encouraging them to articulate their financial aspirations. This collaborative approach ensures that everyone in the family is on the same page and understands the importance of working together towards shared objectives. Setting specific, measurable, achievable, relevant, and time-bound (SMART) goals can further enhance the planning process.

Next, families need to assess their current financial situation. This involves taking stock of income sources, expenses, debts, and assets. Parents can guide their teens in analyzing this information, teaching them how to create a budget that reflects the family's financial landscape. Families can allocate more resources toward their financial goals by reviewing monthly expenditures and identifying areas where spending can be reduced. This exercise helps teens understand the concept of budgeting and highlights the importance of making informed financial decisions based on actual data.

Once the family clearly understands their goals and current financial position, they can develop a strategic plan to achieve those objectives. This may involve creating a savings plan, exploring investment opportunities, or considering entrepreneurial ventures that align with the family's interests. Parents should encourage their teens to think creatively about contributing to the family's financial goals, whether through part-time jobs, starting a small business, or investing in their education. By fostering an entrepreneurial mindset, parents can help their teens recognize the potential for financial growth in various endeavors.

Finally, it is crucial to regularly review and adjust the family's financial plan as circumstances change. Life events such as job changes, unexpected expenses, or shifts in financial goals can impact the family's financial trajectory. Parents should engage their teens in these discussions, emphasizing the importance of adaptability and ongoing financial education. By making financial planning a dynamic process, families can cultivate a culture of financial awareness and responsibility that will benefit both parents and teens in the long run.

Open Conversations About Money

Open conversations about money are essential for fostering financial literacy among teens. Many parents find discussing finances challenging due to their discomfort with the topic. However, initiating these discussions can demystify money management and empower teens to make informed financial decisions. By creating an open dialogue, parents can help their children understand the complexities of money, from budgeting and saving to investing and entrepreneurship. This foundational knowledge can lead to more responsible financial behavior in the future.

One effective way to start these conversations is to share personal money-related experiences. Parents can recount their financial journeys, including successes and mistakes, to illustrate valuable lessons. This approach humanizes the discussion and encourages teens to be open about their financial thoughts and concerns. For instance, parents can talk about how they managed their first job's paycheck or the importance of saving for significant purchases. Such narratives can provide context and make money more relatable for young individuals.

Encouraging teens to set financial goals is another vital aspect of these conversations. Parents can guide their children in identifying short-term and long-term financial objectives, such as saving for a car, funding a college education, or starting a business. Parents can instill a sense of responsibility and motivation by supporting teens in creating actionable plans to achieve these goals. This process teaches teens the value of budgeting and prioritizing their expenses, which are crucial skills in adulthood.

Incorporating discussions about entrepreneurship can also enrich conversations about money. Many teens are interested in starting their own businesses or side hustles. Parents can provide valuable insights into the entrepreneurial journey, including how to identify market opportunities, create business plans, and manage finances. Encouraging teens to explore their interests and turn them into entrepreneurial ventures can help them develop a strong work ethic and financial acumen. This dialogue can also lead to discussions about risk management and the importance of resilience in the face of economic setbacks.

Finally, parents must foster an environment where questions about money are welcomed. Teens should feel comfortable discussing their financial worries, aspirations, and curiosities without fear of judgment. By maintaining an open line of communication and regularly checking in on their teens' financial understanding, parents can ensure their children have the knowledge and confidence needed to navigate the financial world. Open conversations about money ultimately lay the groundwork for a financially savvy generation capable of making informed choices that positively impact their lives.

Teaching by Example

Teaching by example is one of the most potent methods for instilling financial literacy and entrepreneurial spirit in teens. When parents actively demonstrate sound money management practices, they provide a tangible framework for their children to emulate. This approach goes beyond mere lectures or discussions about finances; it incorporates real-life scenarios illustrating the importance of budgeting, saving, and investing. By showcasing their financial habits, parents can create an environment where teens feel empowered to adopt similar practices, leading to a more profound understanding of money.

One effective way to teach by example is through everyday budgeting. Parents can involve their teens in the family's financial planning process, allowing them to see how budgets are created and maintained. Parents can help teens understand the value of prioritizing needs over wants by discussing the rationale behind specific spending decisions. This transparency fosters a sense of responsibility in teens as they learn to track expenses and identify areas where they can save. Moreover, when parents share the goals that come from budgeting, such as saving for a vacation or a new gadget, they illustrate the connection between discipline and achievement.

Investing is another critical area where parents can lead by example. By discussing their own investment choices, whether in stocks, real estate, or retirement accounts, parents can demystify the concept of investing for their teens. They can explain the principles of risk and reward, the importance of diversification, and the benefits of long-term thinking. Engaging teens in conversations about current market trends or involving them in the decision-making process for small investments can spark their interest and encourage them to think strategically about their financial futures.

Entrepreneurship is an exciting avenue for parents to model financial savvy. By sharing their entrepreneurial experiences or encouraging teens to explore their business ideas, parents can illustrate the initiative and creativity required to succeed in this field. Whether starting a lemonade stand, offering tutoring services, or launching an online shop, these experiences can teach valuable lessons about market demand, customer service, and profit. Parents should celebrate successes and failures, emphasizing that each experience provides a learning opportunity that contributes to their financial education.

Finally, open discussions about financial setbacks can be just as instructive as conversations about successes. By sharing their economic challenges and how they overcame them, parents can teach resilience and adaptability. This honesty creates a safe space for teens to express their fears or uncertainties about managing money. Encouraging them to view mistakes as learning experiences fosters a growth mindset essential for personal finance and entrepreneurship. Ultimately, teaching by example equips teens with vital skills and strengthens the parent-child relationship through shared experiences and open dialogue about money management.

CHAPTER 14:
ENCOURAGING
FINANCIAL
INDEPENDENCE

The Path to Financial Independence

The journey to financial independence for teens begins with understanding money management principles. Parents play a crucial role in guiding their children through budgeting, saving, and investing. Teaching teens how to create a budget involves outlining their income sources, such as allowances or part-time jobs, and categorizing expenses. By helping them track their spending, parents can demonstrate the importance of living within their means and making informed financial decisions. Teens need to grasp the concept of prioritizing needs over wants, which lays the groundwork for responsible financial behavior.

As teens gain a grasp of budgeting, the next step is to emphasize the value of saving. Encouraging them to set aside a portion of their income for short-term goals, such as a new gadget or a special outing, fosters a habit of saving that will benefit them in the long run. Parents can introduce the concept of emergency funds, explaining the importance of having savings for unexpected expenses. This practice prepares teens for future financial challenges and instills a sense of security. Additionally, opening a savings account can provide a tangible way for teens to see their savings grow, motivating them to save more.

Investing is another vital component of achieving financial independence. Parents should educate their teens about investment options like stocks, mutual funds, and bonds. Starting with a basic understanding of how the stock market works and the risks involved can empower teens to make informed investment decisions. Moreover, parents can encourage their children to explore investment apps designed for beginners, often providing educational resources. By introducing the principles of compounding interest and the importance of long-term investment strategies, parents can help teens build a foundation for wealth accumulation.

Entrepreneurship is an excellent avenue for teens to explore their financial independence. Encouraging young people to pursue their passions and turn them into business ventures can foster creativity and resilience. Parents can support their teens in brainstorming business ideas, creating business plans, and understanding the business's fundamentals. This hands-on experience teaches practical money management skills and promotes critical thinking and problem-solving abilities. Whether starting a lawn care service, crafting homemade goods, or offering tutoring services, entrepreneurship can provide financial rewards and personal growth.

Finally, fostering a mindset of continuous learning about finance is crucial for long-term financial independence. Parents should encourage their teens to seek resources such as books, podcasts, and online courses focused on personal finance and entrepreneurship. Discussing money management at home can reinforce these concepts and make financial literacy a priority. Parents can help their children cultivate the skills and knowledge necessary to navigate their financial futures confidently by providing ongoing support and encouragement. Ultimately, the path to financial independence is a journey that requires education, practice, and perseverance, all of which can be nurtured within the family unit.

Making Smart Financial Decisions

Making smart financial decisions is crucial for teens navigating the complexities of money management and entrepreneurship. Parents can play a pivotal role in guiding their children to understand the importance of informed financial choices. This begins with instilling a foundational knowledge of budgeting, saving, and spending wisely. Encouraging teens to track their income and expenses can give them a clearer picture of their financial situation, enabling them to make informed decisions about where their money goes.

One effective way to teach teens about financial decision-making is through real-life scenarios. Discussing everyday situations, such as choosing between saving for a desired item or spending impulsively, can open up meaningful conversations. Parents can encourage their teens to weigh each option's pros and cons, helping them understand the long-term implications of their choices. This practice enhances critical thinking skills and fosters a sense of responsibility and accountability regarding personal finances.

Investing is another significant aspect of making intelligent financial decisions. Introducing teens to investing early on can set them up for future financial success. Parents should explain the different types of investments, such as stocks, bonds, and mutual funds, and discuss the benefits of starting to invest at a young age. By encouraging teens to research and consider investments, they can learn about risk management and the potential for compound interest, which can significantly grow their wealth over time.

Entrepreneurship is an exciting avenue for teens to explore financial independence and responsible money management. Parents can support their children by encouraging them to start small businesses or side hustles. This experience teaches valuable lessons about budgeting and revenue generation and promotes creativity and innovation. By guiding them through creating a business plan, understanding costs, and setting realistic financial goals, parents can help their teens develop a strong entrepreneurial mindset.

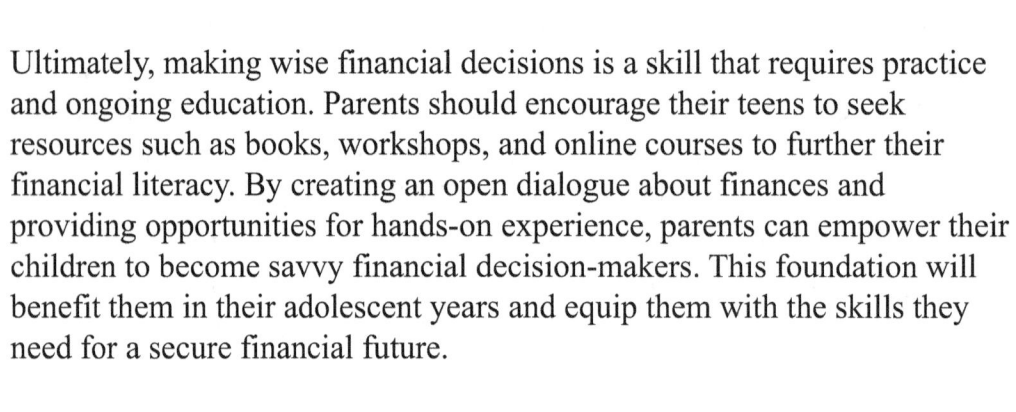

Ultimately, making wise financial decisions is a skill that requires practice and ongoing education. Parents should encourage their teens to seek resources such as books, workshops, and online courses to further their financial literacy. By creating an open dialogue about finances and providing opportunities for hands-on experience, parents can empower their children to become savvy financial decision-makers. This foundation will benefit them in their adolescent years and equip them with the skills they need for a secure financial future.

Preparing for Future Financial Challenges

Preparing for future financial challenges is crucial for parents and teens, as it lays the groundwork for sound money management skills that will last a lifetime. Understanding the importance of financial literacy is the first step in this preparation. Parents should initiate conversations about money management early on, helping their teens grasp fundamental concepts such as budgeting, saving, and investing. This foundational knowledge will empower teens to make informed financial decisions as they grow older and encounter more complex financial situations.

Setting financial goals is an effective strategy for preparing for future challenges. Parents can guide their teens in identifying short-term and long-term goals, such as saving for a new phone, college tuition, or starting a business. By working together to create actionable plans, parents can teach their children the importance of prioritizing needs over wants. This process instills discipline and encourages the development of a growth mindset, enabling teens to adapt to financial obstacles they may face along their financial journey.

Another essential aspect of preparing for financial challenges is understanding the various income-generating opportunities available. Parents can introduce their teens to entrepreneurship by encouraging them to explore side hustles or small business ventures. This hands-on experience helps teens develop a strong work ethic and gives them insights into the realities of managing a business, including budgeting, marketing, and customer service. Parents can help their teens build resilience and confidence in navigating financial uncertainties by fostering an entrepreneurial spirit.

Financial education should extend beyond basic concepts and goal setting. Parents should encourage their teens to engage with more advanced topics, such as investing, credit management, and understanding the implications of loans and debts. Access to books, online courses, or workshops can enhance their understanding of these subjects. By equipping teens with this knowledge, parents can help them make better financial choices, avoiding pitfalls that could lead to long-term financial strain.

Finally, cultivating a mindset of adaptability is vital in preparing for future financial challenges. The financial landscape constantly evolves, influenced by economic shifts, technological advancements, and changing societal norms. Parents should encourage their teens to stay informed about these changes and to be open to adjusting their financial strategies accordingly. Teaching them to view financial challenges as opportunities for growth will empower them to navigate their financial futures with confidence and resilience.

CHAPTER 15:
RESOURCES FOR
CONTINUED LEARNING

Books and Online Courses

Books and online courses are invaluable resources for parents and teens looking to enhance their financial literacy and understanding of entrepreneurship. The wealth of information in books can provide foundational knowledge about money management, investment strategies, and business principles. Parents should take the time to explore various titles that cater specifically to younger audiences, ensuring that the material is engaging and easy to understand. Books such as "The Teen Investor" and "Rich Dad Poor Dad for Teens" offer insights tailored to a teen's perspective, making complex topics more accessible and relatable.

Online courses have gained immense popularity, particularly for their flexibility and interactive nature. Many platforms, such as Coursera, Udemy, and Khan Academy, offer classes specifically designed for young learners. These courses can cover various topics, from personal finance basics to advanced entrepreneurship skills. The interactive elements, such as quizzes, discussions, and project-based assignments, make the learning process more engaging. Parents should encourage their teens to enroll in these courses, as they provide structured learning and can help build valuable skills essential in today's economy.

In addition to traditional learning materials, parents should also seek out books and courses that emphasize real-world application. Resources that include practical exercises, case studies, and projects can significantly enhance a teen's understanding of how to apply financial principles in everyday life. For instance, a course that involves creating a mock business plan or managing a small budget can provide hands-on experience that solidifies theoretical knowledge. Encouraging teens to engage in such activities fosters critical thinking and problem-solving skills crucial for entrepreneurial success.

It is also essential for parents to model a culture of continuous learning within the home. By discussing the books they read or the courses they take, parents can inspire their teens to pursue their educational journeys. This shared experience can lead to meaningful conversations about money management, investments, and entrepreneurship. Parents can also co-enroll in courses with their teens, creating an opportunity for bonding while simultaneously learning about financial literacy together. This collaborative approach not only strengthens family ties but also reinforces the importance of education in achieving financial goals.

Finally, the digital age has made accessing a wealth of information about financial literacy and entrepreneurship easier. Parents should encourage their teens to utilize online resources, such as blogs, podcasts, and webinars, in conjunction with books and courses. These diverse formats can cater to different learning styles and preferences, ensuring teens remain engaged and motivated to learn. By fostering an environment that values education and self-improvement, parents can help their teens develop the skills necessary to navigate the world of finance and entrepreneurship successfully.

Financial Literacy Programs

Financial literacy programs are essential tools designed to equip teens with the knowledge and skills necessary to navigate the complexities of money management. These programs often cover various topics, including budgeting, saving, investing, and understanding credit. By participating in such initiatives, teens can gain practical insights that will serve them well. Understanding financial concepts at an early age can empower them to make informed decisions, ultimately fostering a financially savvy and responsible generation.

Many schools and community organizations offer financial literacy programs tailored specifically for teens. These programs may include workshops, online courses, or interactive seminars. They often include engaging activities and real-world scenarios that resonate with young learners. These programs help teens grasp essential financial concepts more effectively by making the learning process interactive. Parents can encourage their teens to participate in these programs, reinforcing that financial literacy is a vital life skill.

In addition to formal programs, various online resources provide valuable information on financial literacy. Websites, podcasts, and social media channels dedicated to personal finance can be supplementary tools for teens seeking to learn more about managing their money. These platforms often feature relatable content, such as success stories from young entrepreneurs or tips on saving for a big purchase. By exploring diverse resources, teens can find the learning method that best suits their style and preferences, enhancing their understanding of financial principles.

Moreover, parents play a critical role in fostering teen financial literacy. Conversations about money management at home can reinforce the lessons learned in formal programs. Parents can share their experiences with budgeting, saving, and investing, providing real-life examples that resonate with their teens. Encouraging open dialogue about financial goals and challenges can create an environment where teens feel comfortable discussing money matters, ultimately leading to more informed decision-making.

Finally, the impact of financial literacy programs extends beyond individual knowledge; they can inspire teens to pursue entrepreneurship and innovative financial practices. By understanding finance fundamentals, teens may feel more confident in starting their businesses or investing in their ideas. As they learn to manage their finances effectively, they can develop a sense of accountability and ownership over their financial future. This empowerment can lead to a generation of financially literate individuals who are capable of managing their money and eager to create wealth through entrepreneurship.

Community Resources and Workshops

Community resources and workshops play a crucial role in enhancing teens' financial literacy. Parents can explore local libraries, community centers, and schools that often host workshops specifically designed for young people. These workshops cover a variety of topics, such as budgeting, saving, and understanding credit. By utilizing these resources, parents can help their teens gain practical skills essential for managing money effectively. These community programs can also instill confidence in young individuals, empowering them to take charge of their financial futures.

In addition to workshops, many local non-profits and organizations focus on youth entrepreneurship. These entities frequently provide mentorship programs where experienced entrepreneurs share their insights and experiences with teens. Such interactions can inspire young people to explore their entrepreneurial aspirations while learning essential business skills. Parents should actively seek out these opportunities within their communities, as they foster creativity and innovation and teach the importance of resilience and problem-solving in the business world.

Online resources have become increasingly important in today's digital age. Various platforms offer free or low-cost courses for teens interested in money management and entrepreneurship. Websites like Coursera, Khan Academy, and even specific financial literacy platforms provide valuable information and interactive learning experiences. Parents can encourage teens to use these resources, often featuring engaging content tailored to younger audiences. This flexibility allows teens to learn independently and dive deeper into fascinating topics.

Community events and workshops also provide networking opportunities. Parents should encourage their teens to connect with peers and professionals in their fields of interest during these gatherings. Building a network at a young age can open doors to internships, job opportunities, and collaborations that may otherwise be unavailable. These relationships can be invaluable as teens navigate their career paths, providing support, guidance, and resources contributing to their financial literacy and entrepreneurial success.

Finally, parents should consider fostering a culture of continuous learning within the home. Parents can model proactive behavior regarding financial education by discussing the importance of utilizing community resources and attending workshops. They can also participate in workshops with their teens, creating a shared learning experience that strengthens family bonds. This approach reinforces the lessons learned and demonstrates the value of lifelong learning, ensuring that financial literacy becomes a fundamental aspect of their lives moving forward.

www.ingramcontent.com/pod-product-compliance
Lightning Source LLC
Chambersburg PA
CBHW070113230526
45472CB00004B/1240

* 9 7 9 8 3 0 0 0 1 8 8 3 2 *